CW00659569

© OperationReprint All Rights Reserved No part of this book may be reproduced or transmitted in any for or by any means: electronic or mechanical, including photocopying, scanner, recording or by information storage and retrieval system – without permission in writing from the publisher except for the review for inclusion in a magazine, newspaper or broadcast.

For Fancy flies
So very far
When morning
games
Quite merry are

When early dance
And early song
Are very loud
And very long

When all the
room
Is in a stir
There really
is
No place for
her

PENMAWR. FAIRY GLEN

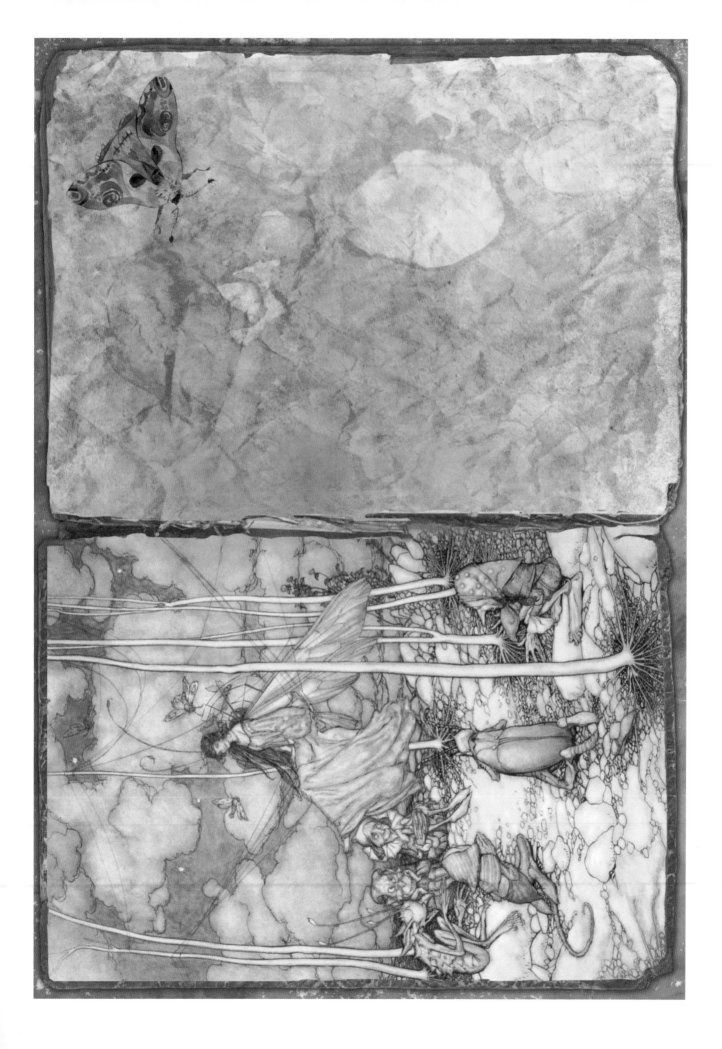

Printed in Great Britain
by Amazon

46929869R10025